WHO DO YOU

choose

TO BE?

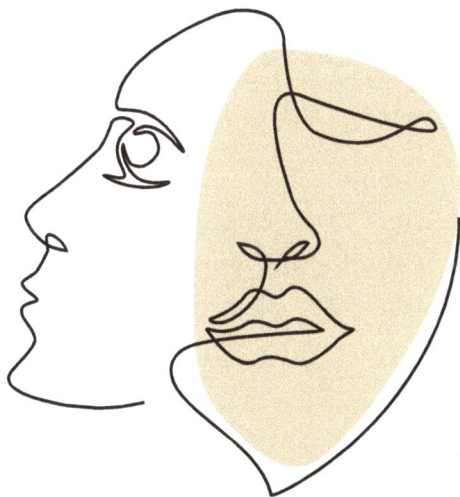

DR PAIGE WILLIAMS

A catalogue record for this book is available from the National Library of Australia

First published in 2026 by Dr Paige Williams, Torquay, Australia. Design and typesetting by Wholehearted Marketing.

For more information about this title, contact:

Dr Paige Williams
paige@drpaige.au
www.drpaige.au

ISBN: 978-0-6486419-2-6 (paperback)

"The sun comes up
and I make a choice
– to rise with it."

Alicia Keys, "Underdog"

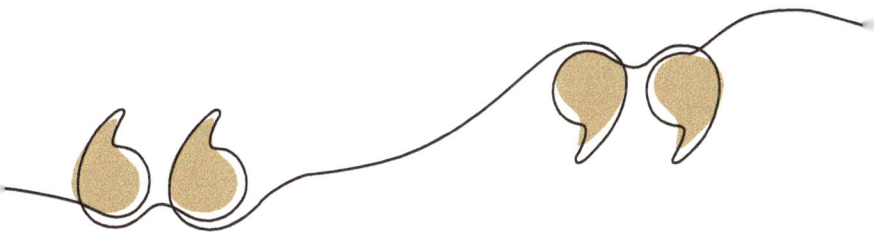

YOUR EXPERIENCE

This book is here to hand you back your choices.

Every day, in ways both small and significant, you are shaping who you are becoming. The real question is – are you doing it consciously?

There's no single way to move through these pages. In fact, I encourage you not to read in order. Start where your attention catches. Sit with the question that won't let you go. Follow the provocation that stirs something awake inside you.

Each chapter is a mirror. A chance to pause, to notice, to choose again. Some reflections may affirm what you already know in your bones. Others may disrupt your certainty or stretch your comfort. Both matter. Growth is rarely neat.

This book is not about fixing. It's about remembering. It's about reclaiming your agency in a world that too often convinces us we have none.

So let these words interrupt you. Let them slow you down. Let them wake you to the truth that every choice leaves a trace – not just in the world around you, but in the person you are becoming.

The invitation is simple. And it's urgent:

Who do you choose to be?

CONTENTS

CHOOSING TO
choose

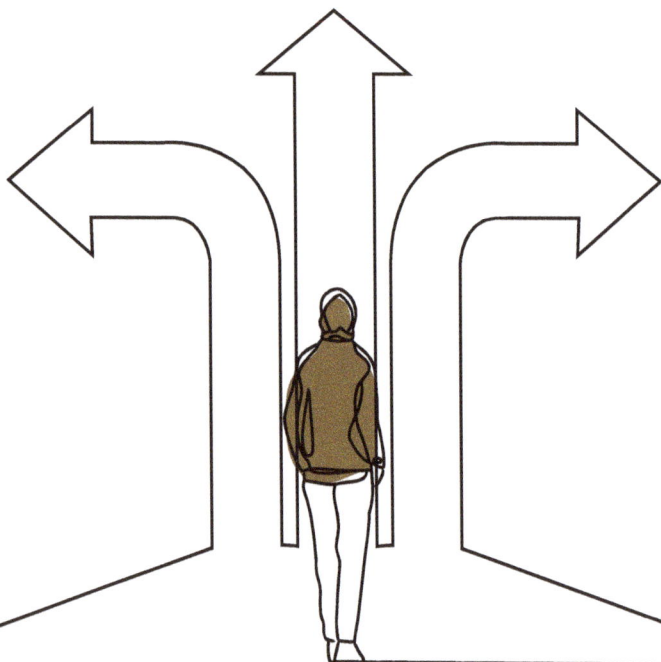

Choice is one of the quiet powers of being human. And yet so often we move through our days forgetting we have it.

Especially when we're tired, stretched thin, or boxed in by responsibilities and expectations. But even in the narrowest corners of our experience, there is still space – sometimes no more than a breath – to choose.

To choose how we show up.

To choose the story we tell ourselves.

To choose what we say yes to – and what we gently but firmly release.

Choice rarely announces itself. It whispers. It hides in the small pivots before reaction. In the decision to take a breath instead of snapping back. In the courage to ask a question instead of collapsing into judgment. In the tenderness that rises when everything in us wants to harden.

When we forget our choices, life carries us along on autopilot – reacting, surviving, performing. When we remember them, we reclaim authorship. We are no longer simply being lived *by* the world – we begin to shape *how we live in it*.

To choose is to remember we are not powerless – it is how we reclaim ourselves.

Where, right now, could you choose differently
– and begin to change the story you are living?

PART I: AWAKENING CHOICE

THERE IS NEVER
NOT A
choice

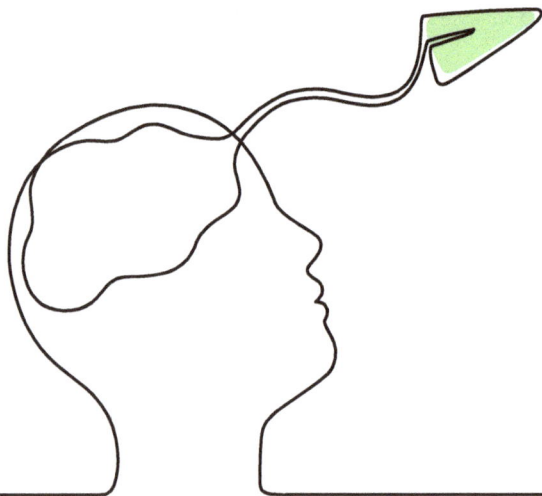

"No choice."

That's the story we tell ourselves when life feels too tight to breathe. When time runs out. When the walls close in and every option seems gone.

But here's the deeper truth: there is never not a choice.

Even in the hardest corners, something remains yours to claim.
Your perspective.
Your next word.
Your breath.
Your stance.
Your refusal to be swallowed by overwhelm.

Choice doesn't always change the circumstances. But it always changes you. It changes how you meet the moment, how you carry yourself through it, how you hold onto what matters.

This isn't about silver linings or forced positivity. It's about agency – reclaimed inch by inch from the grip of helplessness. Agency that says: *I may not control this situation, but I will not abandon myself in it.*

Even the smallest choice pulls you back from the edge and returns you to the centre of your own life.

You may not get to decide what is happening. But you always get to decide how you will respond. And that choice shapes who you are and who you are becoming.

Where have you been telling yourself
there's no choice? What shifts
if you look again?

PART I: AWAKENING CHOICE

choice
-FULL

Life overflows.
Movement, moments, mess, meaning.
And tucked inside it all – choice.

Not only the big, dramatic decisions that shape our direction, but the tiny, almost invisible micro–choices that stitch our days together.

The email we hold back for one more thoughtful read.

The breath we take before reacting.

The smile we offer instead of the sigh we swallow.

Living choice-fully means waking up to these moments. It means refusing to drift through our days half-asleep on autopilot. It's remembering that even in the ordinary, we are constantly co-creating the texture of our lives.

Think of the last time you caught yourself moving through a routine without noticing. Arriving home with no memory of the drive. Nodding in a conversation without really hearing. Choice hides there too – waiting to bring you back to presence.

Even when context feels tight, there is still room to choose – how we show up, what energy we bring, where we place our attention. Choice-full living isn't about control. It's about authorship. About tending what is ours to own, and letting go of the rest.

Living choice-full doesn't ask for more time. It asks for more awareness.

Where in your day is life asking for more intention, more presence, more of *you*?

PART I: AWAKENING CHOICE

CHOOSING NOT TO
choose

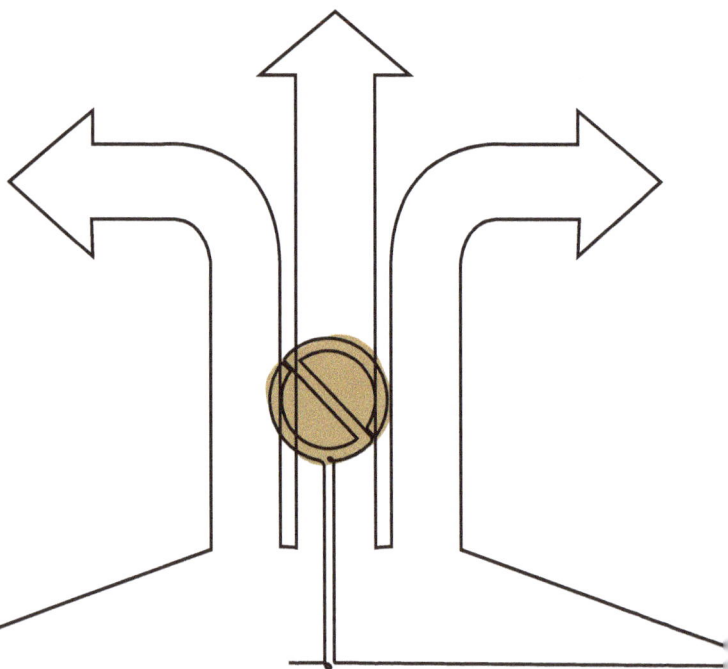

Sometimes the wisest move is no move at all.

We live in a world that rewards speed, decisiveness, clarity. But life is not always ready for our answers. Some moments ask us to wait. To pause. To let the dust settle before we decide what truly matters.

Choosing not to choose is not avoidance – it can be discernment. The discipline of allowing things to unfold in their own time. The wisdom of restraint. The grace of not forcing what is not yet ready.

Stillness has its own strength, silence its own power, and clarity often arrives only after we've stopped trying to push it into being.

Think of the times when waiting brought you more wisdom than rushing ever could. When giving things space revealed a truth you couldn't see in the heat of urgency. That's the quiet courage of not choosing – yet.

We don't always need to fill the gaps with words. We don't always need to rush toward resolution. Sometimes being is enough.

And when the moment for action does arrive, we will meet it with more integrity, more alignment, more truth – because we waited until we could see clearly.

Where in your life is patience the bravest
choice you could make right now?

PART I: AWAKENING CHOICE

"Life shrinks or expands
in proportion
to one's courage."

Anaïs Nin

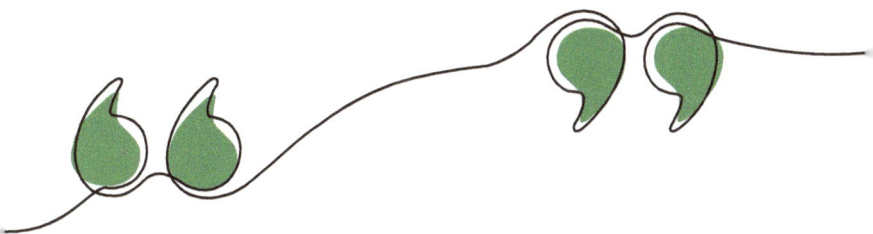

choose

LIFE

Life is not meant to be endured. It's meant to be lived.

To be felt fully. To be shaped intentionally. To be experienced on your own terms.

And yet it's easy to forget that we're allowed to feel good. So much of our energy goes into managing what's expected – meeting obligations, doing the right thing, being responsible. All of this matters, but it can quietly edge out the very things that make life rich: moments of wonder, laughter, awe, connection.

Choosing life is more than getting through the day. It's creating space – on purpose – for what matters most.

To laugh until your body remembers joy.
To feel deeply, even when it's messy.
To do work that fills *you* up, not just your schedule.
To stand with people who see you clearly, and stretch you kindly.
To say no to what depletes, and yes to what brings you alive.

Choosing life doesn't deny hardship. It refuses to let hardship define you. It's the decision to live wide and true, even in the midst of challenge.

You are the designer of your days. You are the one who decides what a full life looks like – for *you*.

What will you add, shift, or release
to choose more *life* in the way you live today?

PART II: CHOOSING TO LIVE FULLY

choosing

LOVE

Love takes courage.

It isn't always soft. Sometimes it is the fiercest, most radical choice we can make.

Not just romantic love – though that matters too.
But big love.
Agape love.
The kind that stretches us wider than we thought possible. The kind that holds complexity when we'd rather retreat into certainty. The kind that refuses to shut down, even when life gets hard.

To choose love is to declare:
I will stay present.
I will stay open.
I will meet this moment – this person, this challenge, this part of myself – with generosity and care.

It's easy to love when things are light and flowing. The real invitation is to love when it costs us something. When it's inconvenient. When it stretches us beyond what we thought we could give.

To love life – especially when it's messy or uncertain – is an act of defiance. It's choosing to see beauty in the breakdown. To honour the whole spectrum of human experience, not just the curated highlights. To remember that tenderness is not weakness, but strength woven through with courage.

Choosing love is about willingness. To be moved. To be changed. To keep your heart open when everything in you wants to close.

What would choosing love
ask of you right now?

PART II: CHOOSING TO LIVE FULLY

NO IS A
choice
TOO

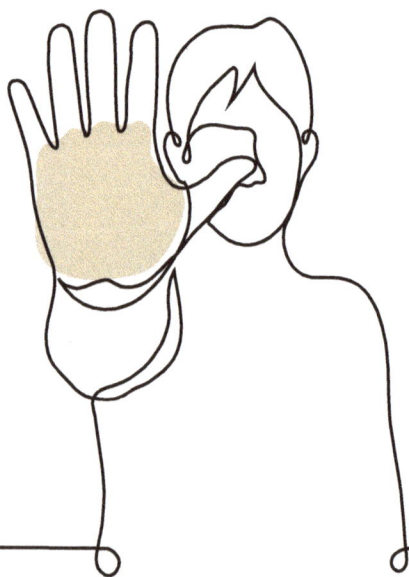

We often celebrate the power of *yes*. But some of the most important choices in our lives are the ones where we say *no*.

No to overcommitting.
No to people–pleasing at the expense of ourselves.
No to patterns that keep us small, stuck, or safe.

Saying no isn't selfish – it can be one of the clearest forms of self-respect. And yet it rarely feels simple. *No* can stir guilt, discomfort, even disapproval. Especially when you've been the steady one, the reliable one, the one who always says *yes*.

But here's the truth: every *yes* that isn't aligned is a quiet *no* to yourself.

When you choose no – with clarity and compassion – you mark a boundary that says: *I honour my energy. I know my limits. I trust my wisdom.*

No is not rejection of others. It is recognition of self. It is the space that restores meaning to *yes*.

A *no* can be the pause that protects your purpose.
The breath that safeguards your peace.
The line that helps you live in alignment, not exhaustion.

Where in your life would a clear, courageous *No* become the choice that sets you free?

PART II: CHOOSING TO LIVE FULLY

A CURIOUS
choice

Curiosity isn't a personality trait – it's a practice. And like every practice, it begins with a choice.

A choice to wonder instead of assume, to ask instead of label, to listen instead of conclude.

Curiosity invites us to meet the world with a beginner's mind: open, spacious, willing to be surprised. It loosens our grip on certainty and creates space for connection where judgment might otherwise shut things down.

It's easy to be curious when nothing is on the line. It's harder when the temperature rises – when someone says something you strongly disagree with, or when your own biases flare. In those moments, curiosity is not just gentle; it's radical.

To choose curiosity is to say: *I'm willing to learn what I don't yet see or understand.* It disarms defensiveness. It builds bridges across difference. It shifts the question from "What's wrong with them?" to "What might I be missing?"

You don't have to agree to be curious. You only have to stay present. Because curiosity doesn't close doors – it holds them open.

Where are you being asked to pause your
certainty and make the braver choice
to stay curious?

PART II: CHOOSING TO LIVE FULLY

"The privilege of a lifetime is to become who you are."

C.G. Jung

BECOMING THROUGH
choice

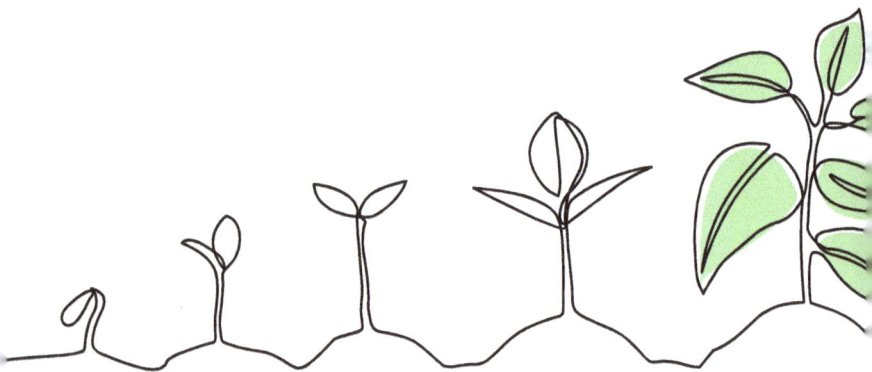

Every choice leaves a trace. Not just in the world around us, but in the person we are becoming.

The small ones.
The unseen ones.
The brave ones.
The reluctant ones.

Each decision shapes us. Every act is part of the slow work of becoming.

Moment by moment, choice by choice, we are always in motion:

Becoming more aligned... or less.
More open... or more defended.
More whole... or more performative.

This is about direction over perfection.

Because choosing is never only about options. It is about identity. It is how we embody our values. How we reveal what matters. How we claim – or reclaim – the person we are here to be.

And the truth is, we are not fixed. We can choose again. We can evolve. We can grow forward.

Every yes, every no, every pause, every pivot – each one writes us into being.

So the question isn't just *what will you choose?*
It is: *Who are you becoming through your choices?*

Is the person you are becoming
the version of you that feels most true?

PART III: CHOOSING TO BE YOU

choosing

TO BE REAL

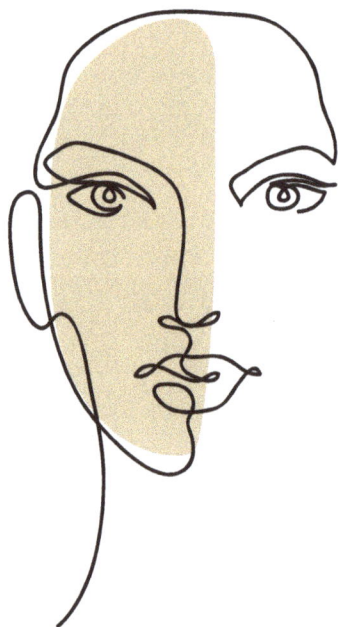

There's a pressure – especially in leadership – to perform.
To present the version of ourselves we think others want to see.
To polish the rough edges.
To package what's acceptable instead of revealing what's true.

But performance gets heavy. And eventually, the cost of the mask becomes greater than the risk of removing it.

Choosing to be real isn't about spilling every thought or oversharing in the name of honesty. It's about alignment. About letting the inside match the outside. About refusing to contort ourselves to fit expectations that were never ours to begin with.

The mask is built slowly – layer by layer. A compromise here, a silence there, a smile that hides what we really feel. At first, it protects us. But over time, it distances us from ourselves. And when we're distant from ourselves, connection with others becomes shallow too.

Being real means telling the truth – first to ourselves, then to others. It means holding our power with humility and our uncertainty with grace. It means being willing to feel awkward, exposed, even misunderstood... and doing it anyway.

Because real creates resonance.
Real builds trust.
And real is the only sustainable foundation for a life, a culture, or a legacy worth leaving.

What part of you is asking to be seen more fully? What would it mean to choose real, even if it feels risky?

PART III: CHOOSING TO BE YOU

choosing

TO BE SEEN

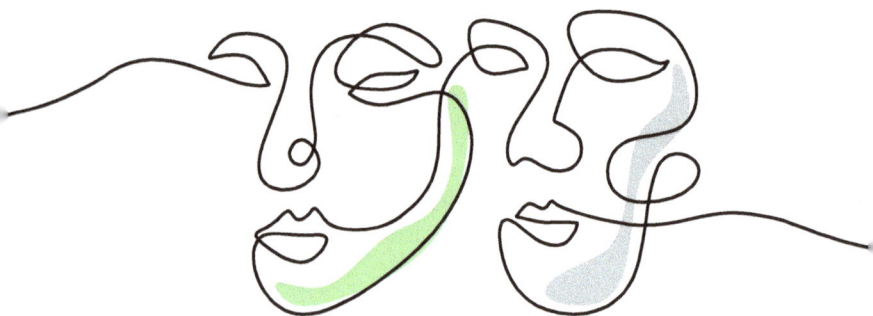

Being seen isn't always about standing out.
It's about letting in – allowing yourself to be witnessed.
Not for what you've achieved.
Not for the version you've curated.
But for who you truly are, here and now.

Choosing to be seen is rarely loud. It can be as simple as staying open when everything inside you wants to shut down. As subtle as letting a compliment land instead of brushing it away. As brave as allowing someone to meet you in your mess, not only in your strength.

To be seen is to lower the armour, even just a little. To let love, feedback, and connection find you without flinching or deflecting. That's why it can feel so risky: many of us learned to hide early, to protect our softest places from judgment or rejection. Hiding may keep us safe, but it also keeps us lonely.

This is about worth, not performance. Receptivity, not control. Presence, not polish.

Being seen doesn't mean revealing everything. It means no longer concealing what longs to be known.

Because when we allow ourselves to be seen, we create a bridge. We show others that vulnerability is survivable – and that connection is possible.

Where are you ready to soften your edges
and allow yourself to be seen – fully,
and without defence?

PART III: CHOOSING TO BE YOU

choosing

TO BE MORE THAN ONE THING

We're often asked to simplify ourselves.
Pick a lane.
Stick to a title.
Stay consistent.

But real people don't live in tidy boxes. We are layered, evolving, and at times even contradictory. And that isn't a flaw – it's a richness.

Choosing to be more than one thing means letting your complexity be seen. You can be strong *and* tender. Analytical *and* intuitive. Still learning *and* already wise. These aren't contradictions to resolve; they are truths to embrace.

You don't owe anyone a streamlined version of yourself. You don't need to perform predictability to be taken seriously. And you don't need to shrink to one note when you were born to be a symphony. Each part of you – every instrument, every variation – adds depth to the whole.

The world may try to flatten you into a label or a role. But each time you resist that pressure, you expand what is possible. You show others they can bring more of themselves too.

This is identity as wholeness.
This is leadership that includes nuance.
This is culture shaped by authenticity, not conformity.

Being more than one thing is not indulgent. It's honest. It's generous. And it's the only sustainable way to lead, live, and love.

What part of you could open if you
let it live out loud?

PART III: CHOOSING TO BE YOU

choosing

TO BELONG
(WITHOUT LOSING YOUSELF)

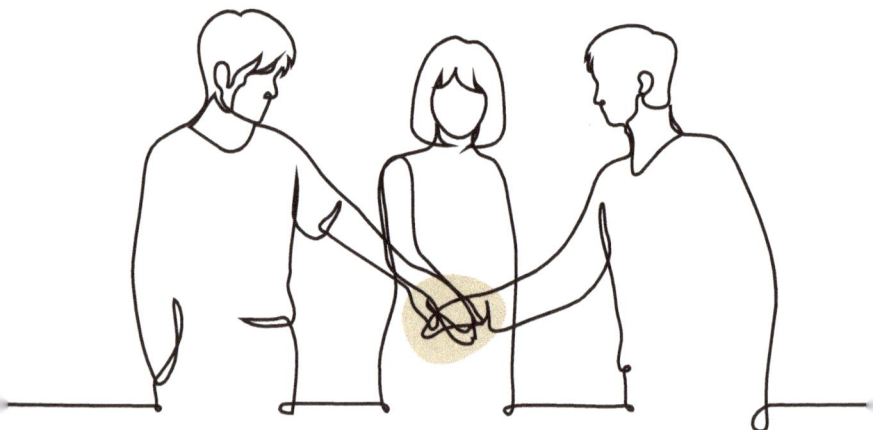

We all long to belong.
To be part of something.
To feel seen, accepted, valued.

But in our effort to fit in, we can start to disappear. We edit ourselves to match the room. We perform certainty to avoid standing out. We trade authenticity for approval – and slowly, the cost of being accepted becomes losing ourselves.

Choosing to belong without losing yourself means staying rooted in who you are, even as you reach toward others. It's the courage to speak up when silence would be safer. To hold your difference when sameness seems the easier path. To remember that belonging isn't about blending – it's about being real.

True belonging doesn't ask for your sameness. You don't have to fragment to be welcome. You don't have to shrink to be included.

And when you bring your full, unedited self into the room, you create the conditions for others to do the same. Inclusive cultures are not built only by who's invited, but by who feels safe enough to stay whole once they arrive.

Belonging is not about permission – it's about truth.

Where in your life are you ready to stop fitting in and begin belonging, fully and freely?

PART III: CHOOSING TO BE YOU

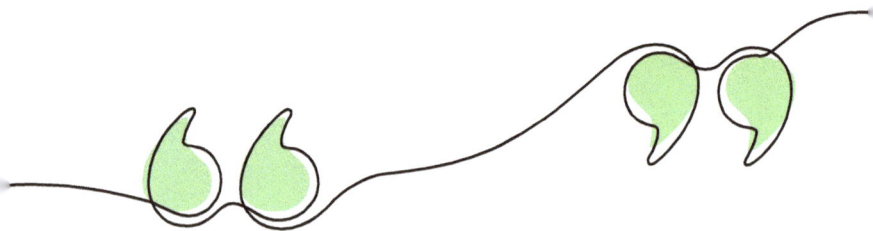

"No one can build you the
bridge on which you,
and only you, must cross
the river of life."

Friedrich Nietzsche

choosing
TO BE IN RELATIONSHIP

We don't exist in isolation.
Even our most personal choices ripple outward, shaping the lives around us.

Choosing to be in relationship means taking responsibility not only for ourselves, but for how we show up in connection. It means recognising that the quality of our relationships is inseparable from the quality of our presence within them.

To be in relationship is to ask:
Can I stay open when I feel misunderstood?
Can I hold space without rushing to fix?
Can I listen deeply – even when I don't agree?

Being in relationship invites us to bring our whole selves forward with integrity and care. To hold boundaries alongside compassion. To practice honesty with humility. To lean into courage with curiosity.

It also asks us to stay when it's easier to withdraw. To choose repair over resentment. To allow difference without letting it become distance.

We don't get to control how others respond. But we do get to choose how we engage – with respect, with clarity, with the hope that showing up wholeheartedly creates more room for wholeness us both.

Relationship is rarely ease alone. It is the ongoing practice of choosing connection in the midst of complexity.

Who do you choose to be in your relationships, especially when the ease has gone?

PART IV: CHOOSING IN CONNECTION

choosing

TO BE WITH DIFFERENCE

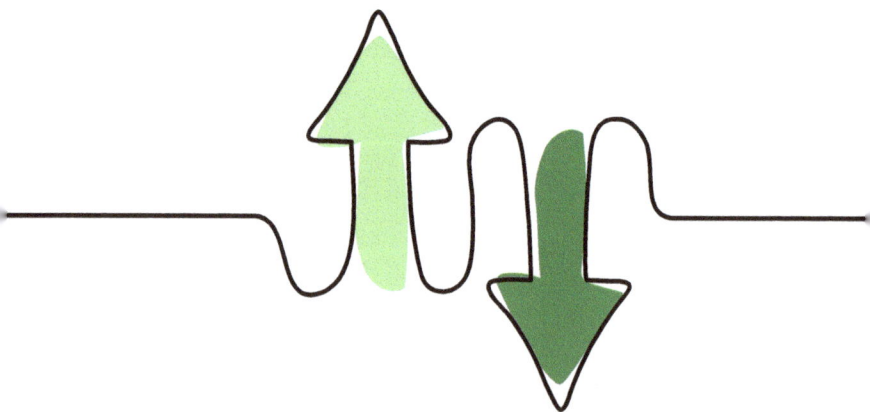

Difference can be uncomfortable.
It unsettles our assumptions, disrupts our certainty, stretches the edges of our worldview.
Which is exactly why it matters.

Choosing to be with difference means resisting the urge to collapse it – to fix it, silence it, explain it away, or convert it into something more familiar. Instead, it asks us to stay open, present, connected.

To be with difference is to acknowledge that your experience is not the only truth. That other ways of seeing, being, knowing, and doing can be equally valid – even when they feel foreign, inconvenient, or confronting.

This is more than tolerance. Tolerance keeps difference at arm's length. This is respect. Humility. A choice to hold space for perspectives that challenge your own – and to trust that doing so makes us all more whole.

Because without difference, there is no innovation. No resilience. No real inclusion. Only the fragile surface of sameness.

Being with difference means leading beyond comfort. It means widening your perspective, loosening your grip on being right, and choosing growth over certainty.

It's not easy work. But it is necessary work – because difference is the raw material of transformation.

Where are you being invited to stretch,
not by changing others, but by letting
their difference expand you?

PART IV: CHOOSING IN CONNECTION

choosing

TO BE THE BRIDGE

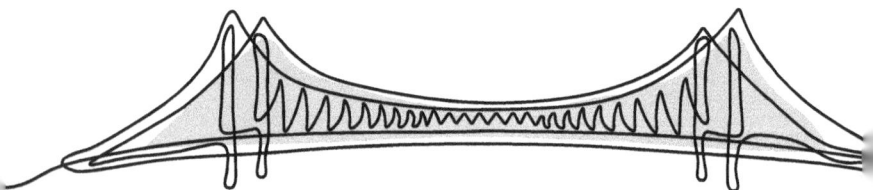

In polarised spaces, it's easy to pick a side.
It's harder – and braver – to stand in between.

Choosing to be the bridge means holding the tension without collapsing into one view or the other. It means recognising the humanity in both, and seeing possibility where others see only opposition. *That* becomes your ground.

To be the bridge is not to be neutral. It is to be connected. To keep relationships open while others shut down. To stay curious where certainty feels safer. To hold dialogue steady even when disagreement sharpens.

This work is rarely visible, and even less often rewarded. You may feel misunderstood. You may feel alone. Yet in your presence, others find enough safety to risk reaching across.

To be the bridge is to be the one who stays.
Stays in the discomfort.
Stays in dialogue.
Stays in service of something larger than agreement: *understanding*.

It takes strength to hold both ends without snapping. It takes self-trust to stand firm in the middle. And it takes vision to keep inviting others across – not to erase difference, but to weave connection through it.

Where might your presence become
the bridge – not just between people,
but between what is and what could be?

PART IV: CHOOSING IN CONNECTION

choosing

TO UPLIFT

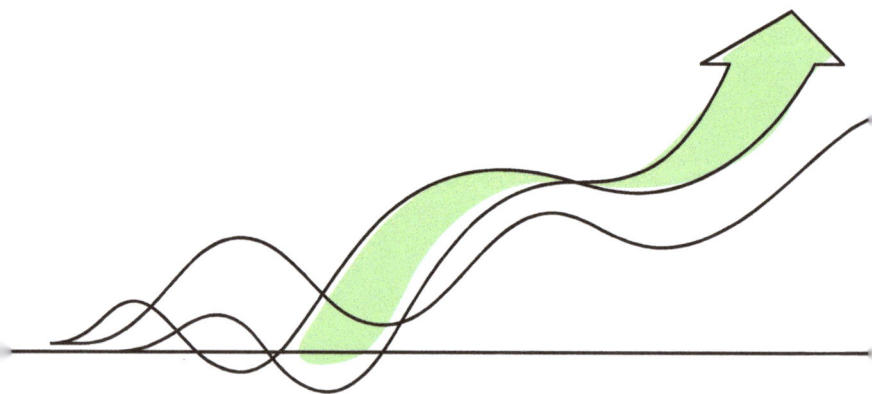

In a world wired for competition, choosing to uplift is a quiet act of rebellion.
It's the choice to celebrate instead of compare.
To share power instead of protect it.
To advocate, elevate, and believe in someone – sometimes even before they believe in themselves.

To uplift is not to rescue. It's to hold others in their strength. To reflect their potential back to them, especially when they can't yet see it clearly. It's a way of saying: *I see you. I trust you. I believe in what you carry.*

Choosing to uplift doesn't always look grand. It might mean stepping aside so someone else can shine. Naming someone's contribution in a room where they're not present. Asking, "Whose voice is missing?" – and making space for it to be heard.

This is not performative allyship. This is relational leadership. A commitment to equity, dignity, and mutual rising.

When we uplift, we interrupt scarcity. We replace comparison with connection. We create cultures where trust can take root and where people feel safe enough to bring their whole selves forward.

Because uplifting others doesn't diminish you. It deepens you and strengthens us all.

Where might your presence, encouragement, or platform be the very thing that helps someone rise?

PART IV: CHOOSING IN CONNECTION

choosing

TO LEAD TOGETHER

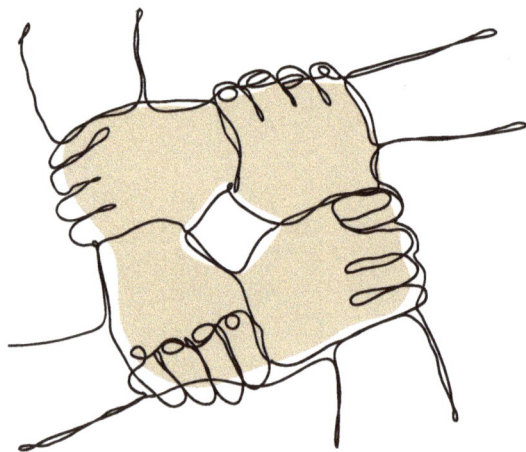

Leadership is a team sport.

It's not about being the hero, the fixer, or the one with all the answers.

It's about holding space for others to rise – alongside you, not behind you.

Choosing to lead together means loosening grip on control and choosing collaboration over command. It's the shift from "How do I lead others?" to "How do we lead this – together?"

This kind of leadership asks for more than expertise. It asks for trust. For shared power. For the humility to let go of ego and the courage to lean into collective wisdom.

It's not always neat. Collaboration can be slower. Messier. More complex. But it's also more resilient. More human. More future-fit.

When we lead together, we stop performing leadership as a solo act and start practising it as a shared art. We bring real people, in all their diversity and brilliance, into the centre of the work.

And when that happens, something shifts.. People don't just follow. They contribute. They co-create. They take ownership. They grow into leaders in their own right.

This is leadership that scales. Not through control, but through trust. Not through hierarchy, but through shared strength.

Where might you loosen your grip,
share the load, and lead more powerfully,
by leading together?

PART IV: CHOOSING IN CONNECTION

"You can't heal what you hide;
you can't grow
where you don't go."

H.E.R., "As I Am"

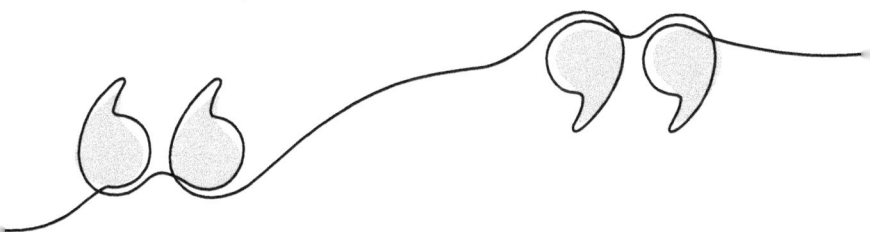

A DIFFERENT
choice

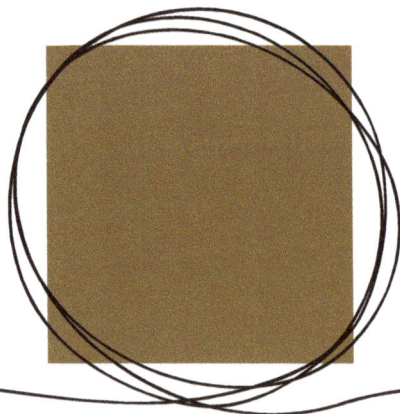

Some of the most powerful moments in life come when we dare to be different.

When we stop asking, *How do I fit in?*

And start asking, *What needs to shift?*

Choosing different means we don't follow the rules just because they exist. We pause long enough to ask: Do these rules serve us – or do they keep us small, safe, stuck?

To choose differently is to make space for what's exceptional –
In ourselves.
In others.
In the systems we live and lead within.

Sameness is easy to reward. But real inclusion – the kind that expands us all – depends on difference. On the edge-walkers. On the truth-speakers. On those willing to hold their shape, even when it would be easier to shrink.

This isn't rebellion for attention's sake. It's the courage to honour what's true, even when it's inconvenient or misunderstood.

Every time we choose different, we give others permission to do the same. We make it safer for what's real to rise and we shift cultures – not through statements and slogans, but through the courage of our choices.

Where are you being called to break the rules to break through and what might that open up for others?

PART V: CHOOSING COURAGE

choosing
TO BE THE DISRUPTION

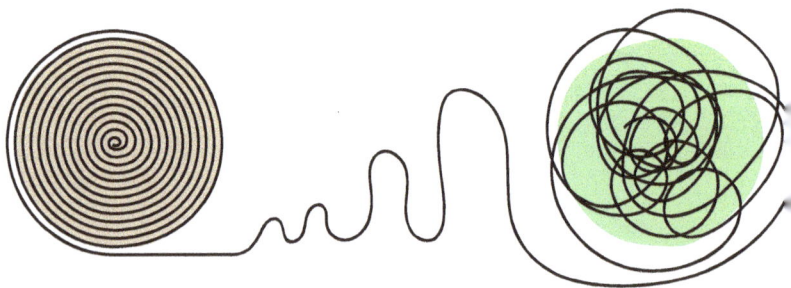

Sometimes the most courageous act is to interrupt what's not working.
The meeting where silence masks fear.
The system where the loudest voices dominate.
The culture where busyness is a badge and burnout is the cost.

Choosing to be the disruption means noticing what isn't being said – and daring to name it. It means stepping in when others step back. Staying with the discomfort long enough for something new to emerge.

This is not disruption for attention's sake. It's disruption in service of truth. Of equity. Of possibility.

And it comes with a cost. You may not be thanked for it. You may feel misunderstood, even isolated. You might question whether the silence would have been easier. But change never begins with consensus. It begins with someone willing to see clearly – and to speak anyway.

To be the disruption is to trust that discomfort is not danger. It is data. It is a doorway. It is the ground from which growth takes root.

Because disruption isn't destruction. Done with courage and care, it is an act of imagination. A conscious break from what limits, so that something healthier can take hold.

Where are you being called to disrupt
to reimagine what's possible?

PART V: CHOOSING COURAGE

choosing

TO BE THE FIRST

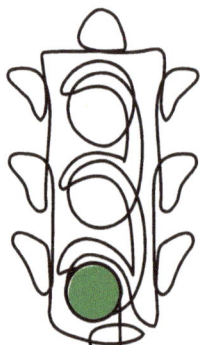

Someone has to go first.
To name what's unspoken.
To take the first step down a path no one has yet cleared.
To risk being seen so others can risk following.

Choosing to be the first isn't about being the best or the bravest. It's about being willing. Willing to step in even when your voice shakes. Willing to model what's possible – even if your hands are still trembling.

To go first is to lead without a map. To stand in uncertainty when the outcome is unclear and the stakes are real. It is choosing momentum over mastery, trusting that clarity will come through action, not before it.

Sometimes you'll be met with silence. With raised eyebrows, resistance, or doubt. That doesn't mean you're wrong. It means you're early.

And you may never see the full ripple of what your courage sets in motion. But your willingness to go first disrupts inertia. It signals that movement is safe, possible, allowed. It opens the doorway for others to follow through.

This is how change begins: with someone willing to say, *"I'll go."*

Where are you being asked to go first –
not because it's easy, but because it's needed?

PART V: CHOOSING COURAGE

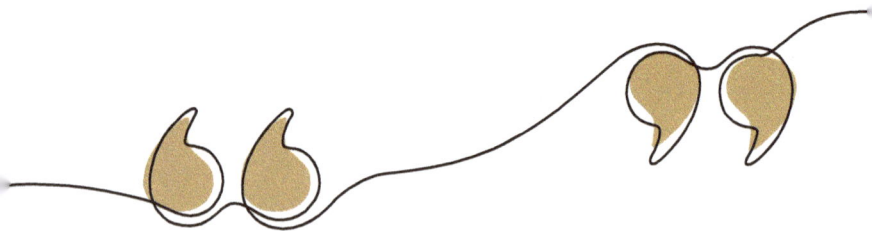

"Nothing ever goes away
until it has taught us
what we need to know."

Pema Chödrön

choosing

TO BE WITH IT

Not everything needs fixing. Not every feeling requires an explanation. Not every hard thing is waiting for a solution.

Sometimes the bravest thing we can do is stay.
Stay with the discomfort.
Stay with the silence.
Stay with what is.

Choosing to be with it means resisting the reflex to rush in and rescue. It's the pause that lets the truth land. The willingness to hold space for others – even when we can't hold answers. The courage to sit with our own complexity without trying to resolve it too soon.

This is not passivity. It is power.

To be with it – whatever "it" is – is to stay in relationship with reality, with ourselves, and with others as we face it together. Not denying. Not distracting. Not deflecting.

It asks for presence instead of performance. Curiosity instead of certainty. Compassion instead of control.

When we stay with what's real, we create space for transformation. Not because we pushed it into being, but because we allowed it to arrive.

Where are you being asked to stay a little longer – with it, in it, alongside it – rather than move to action too soon?

PART VI: CHOOSING RENEWAL & LEGACY

choosing

TO BEGIN AGAIN

We all falter.

Say the wrong thing. Miss the moment. Break our own rules. We all know what it feels like to fall short of who we want to be.

But the real question is: *what happens next?*

Choosing to begin again is choosing growth over guilt. It's recognising the moment you drifted off-course and choosing to return with intention. The quiet act of reclaiming your integrity, one small step at a time.

To begin again doesn't mean erasing the past. It means letting it inform your next move without letting it define your worth. It means making space for repair, for forgiveness, for learning. It's about becoming more aligned, not perfect.

This choice is rarely flashy. Often, it's private. Humbling. Unseen by anyone else. Yet it's also how we rebuild self-trust. How we restore connection. How we return to what matters – again and again and again.

Because you don't have to get it right the first time. Or every time. You just need to be willing to come back. To start where you are, as you are, and choose again.

Where in your life or your leadership are you being invited to begin again?

PART VI: CHOOSING RENEWAL & LEGACY

choosing

THE FUTURE YOU
WANT TO LEAVE

Every choice we make leaves a trace.
In our relationships.
In our communities.
In the culture we're shaping – whether we realise it or not.

Choosing the future you want to leave isn't just about long-term planning or the stories people might tell when you're gone. It's about present-tense integrity. About living today in a way your future self – and those who come after you – would be proud of.

This is bigger than legacy as performance. This is legacy as alignment. It's found in what you protect, what you amplify, what you give your energy to, and what you quietly refuse to normalise.

You may never see the full impact of who you've been. But someone will benefit from the boundaries you held. From the truth you spoke. From the compassion you offered in a moment when it would have been easier to close down.

The future is not fixed. We don't control it. But we do influence it, moment by moment, through how we choose to show up now.

Every yes, every no, every act from truth is a thread in the tapestry of tomorrow.

What kind of future are you choosing,
through your presence, your practice,
and your everyday decisions today?

PART VI: CHOOSING RENEWAL & LEGACY

"With every breath,
life invites our participation.

In every decision,
we leave a trace.

To choose is to create our story –
to align intention with action,
to remember that becoming
is a lifelong art.

Every choice a brushstroke,
a quiet declaration
of who we are and
who we are still becoming.

And when we choose with love,
with courage,
with consciousness,
we become
the kind of person
the future can trust."

Dr Paige Williams

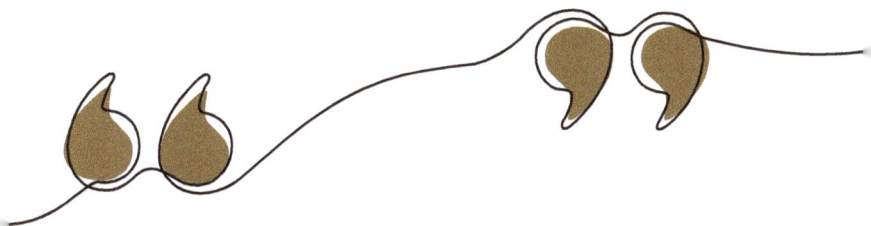

ABOUT THE AUTHOR

Dr Paige Williams is an author, researcher and PhD in Organisational Behaviour. A trusted advisor and mentor to senior leaders across business, government, education and beyond, she uses a potent blend of neuroscience, psychology and her own twenty-plus years of international business leadership experience to surface uncomfortable truths and help leaders see the rules they need to break in order to breakthrough and lead themselves, their teams, and their organisations to thrive.

The results are dramatic and measurable.

www.ingramcontent.com/pod-product-compliance
Lightning Source LLC
Chambersburg PA
CBHW040928210326
41597CB00030B/5220